Amazon FBA

Complete Guide to Amazon FBA Success A-Z

Jason Cooper

Copyright © 2017 Jason Cooper

All rights reserved. No part of this book may be reproduced or transmitted in any form or by any means, electronic or mechanical, including photocopying, recording or by any information storage and retrieval system without written permission of the publisher, except for the inclusion of brief quotations in a review.

Table of Contents

INTRODUCTION 1
CHAPTER 1: ABOUT AMAZON FBA 2
CHAPTER 2: CHOOSING A PRODUCT 7
CHAPTER 3: MANAGING YOUR PRODUCT 29
CHAPTER 4: MARKETING STRATEGIES 36
CHAPTER 5: GATHERING FEEDBACK 40
CHAPTER 6: SUPPLIER RELATIONSHIPS 42
CONCLUSION 51

Amazon Fba

Introduction

Thank you for purchasing "*Amazon FBA*: Complete Guide to Amazon FBA". This guide was carefully created to help you master Amazon FBA in the process of reading this. You will learn about exactly what Amazon FBA is, how you can choose products that will earn you profit, all you need to know about marketing and suppliers, and so much more.

Amazon FBA is an incredible platform for people to open online businesses and start making a profit. It is a great way to generate income, even passive incomes if you set yourself up properly! With this book, you will learn to do anything you want to do with your Amazon FBA business, and earn as much as you want to earn.

While it may seem mysterious and difficult now, by the end of this book you will be a master at Amazon FBA. You will be able to do anything within your Amazon FBA business that you desire, or even outsource it to increase the passivity of your income stream.

If you are ready to start earning major income from your new Amazon FBA business, then read on!

Amazon Fba

Chapter 1: About Amazon FBA

Amazon FBA means "Fulfillment by Amazon". In other words, you run your business and Amazon stores your inventory and ships it to respective buyers. This incredible business opportunity opens you up for the ability to develop a completely passive business if you so desire. You can stay involved in your business, or you can outsource everything and turn it into a passive income stream. The choice is yours!

In this chapter, you are going to explore exactly what Amazon FBA has to offer you and your online business. You will learn about what lies within' your responsibility, and what Amazon is offering to fulfill for you. As a result, you will know exactly what you need to do to keep your business growing at exponential rates.

The Amazon FBA Opportunity

Amazon FBA is a program put on by Amazon that makes it incredibly easy for online merchants to run lucrative businesses with minimal work. The opportunity offered by Amazon makes it incredibly easy for you, as the merchant, to have your inventory and shipping processes covered. Additionally, being an Amazon FBA merchant gives you access to several other sweet bonuses offered by Amazon. They are as follows:

Free Two-Day Shipping
Merchants who ship through Amazon FBA have guaranteed access to free two-day shipping. That means that all of their orders will be sent out within' two days of the order being placed by a Prime customer at no extra cost to the merchant or the customer. Amazon FBA enables all members who are Amazons Prime members to take advantage of all of the Prime features available within' merchants. This extra shipping is free to you as well, as it comes at no additional cost for what you are already paying for your Amazon FBA membership.

Access to International Marketplace
Amazon offers an international marketplace for you to ship to, and when you ship with Amazon FBA you get access to that marketplace without having to worry about varying shipping costs. Instead, Amazon takes care of that for you! Whether you want to ship to Canada, the United States, Mexico, or anywhere within' North America. This increases your product reach and gives you even more opportunity to sell, with a higher number of potential buyers who may be interested in your products.

Amazon Oversees Customer Service and Returns
When you ship with Amazon FBA, Amazon takes over the responsibility for seeing to your customer service and returns associated with your products and shipments. This means that

all you really have to do is pick products, manage production and manage your product listings. Everything else associated with the product and shipments is managed by Amazon.

A Prime Logo

All Amazon FBA merchants are provided with the exclusive Amazon Prime logo on their listings. This means that Amazon Prime members who are shopping for your products will know right away that they get access to all of their sweet membership-exclusive opportunities with your product listings. It is just like having a business-exclusive membership without having to oversee the membership program or processes!

Speedy Growth Opportunities

Since Amazon FBA oversees a great deal of the work involved with managing your products and shipping, it takes a lot of work off of you. That means that you can simply focus on choosing products and having them produced and sent to an Amazon FBA warehouse for Amazon to do the rest. Without you having to worry about *so much* of the business processes, you can focus more on the development of your business and getting the word out there! That means you can grow your business quickly and with minimal effort on your own behalf!

Multi-Channel Fulfillment Opportunity

With multi-channel fulfillment, you can advertise your products all over the internet marketplace and have all of the orders fulfilled by Amazon. That means that you are not forced to only sell on the Amazon website. Instead, you can place your unique products for sale anywhere using Amazon's unique multi-channel fulfillment features, and Amazon will fulfill the orders

Amazon Fba

no matter what website they're ordered from!

Easy, Cost Effective Business Model

When you are running a brick and mortar business, you have to worry about a significant amount of overhead. When you are running a regular online business, you still have a great deal of overhead when you factor in inventory storage and shipping costs. However, when you have an Amazon FBA business, your cost reduces significantly. Instead of paying for each individual shipment, and to store all of your products, you get to pay a single fee for all of this.

Additionally, Amazon has a sweet opportunity where you only pay for the exact amount of storage you are using to store your products. So, if that is less in some months than it is in others, then you will save money during those months! As well, you will not be charged any extra for having access to Amazon's free two-day shipping, or anything else. It's a great opportunity to save money on your business overhead and make more profit, as well as focus more on business growth. Ultimately, it's extremely easy to expand your Amazon FBA business rapidly and turn it into a highly profitable income stream in a short time period!

Inventory Storage and Shipping Services

As you have likely already gathered, the biggest benefit to Amazon FBA is that you have your storage covered and your shipping services covered. You do not have to worry about storing your products or ensuring that they are stored safely and appropriately. You do not have to worry about paying for larger storage lockers whenever your inventory levels grow, or paying extra for storage space you are not using on months when you have less inventory. You also don't have to worry about paying the enormous tab that comes with running a shipment business.

In addition to all of the money you save, you also save valuable time. It can take a lot of work to receive and store shipments of products, and then wrap them and ship them out to their buyers. With all of that time you save, you can invest it in growing your business, or doing anything else that you desire! It is a win-win situation!

Amazon FBA is an incredible and powerful business opportunity for anyone who is looking to have a business online. You have the opportunity to rapidly grow your business, save enormous amounts of time and money, and have a great deal of your business operations outsourced to a reliable company. You gain tons of added value with being seen on an international marketplace that offers unique memberships for buyers, giving you a number of benefits to provide for your customers as well as your own business. You really can't go wrong with Amazon FBA and all that it has to offer!

Chapter 2: Choosing A Product

In order to be an Amazon FBA merchant, you're going to need something to sell! There are a few ways that you can discover items to sell, and then some information you should know about having your orders fulfilled by suppliers! In this chapter, you are going to discover exactly how you can discover which products are best for you to sell, and how you can start ordering those products really quick!

Discovering Your Product

Figuring out what product you want to sell is something that you really need to focus on when you are getting started as an Amazon FBA merchant. It doesn't take long to discover what product you want to sell, but you will need to invest some time and energy into picking the right products. It is recommended that you perform the following checks for about five to ten products at a time, as you will end up ruling some products out along the way. Doing several at a time will help ensure you end up with at least one good product, if not several that you can choose from and a list you can use for your expansion plans.

The Top 100

A great way to figure out what products are going to sell for you is to start looking at the top 100 lists on Amazon. Look at the top 100 products selling on Amazon altogether, and look at the top 100 list for your unique category. The more you learn, the better. These products are ones that are definitely selling, despite there being hundreds of thousands of products available on Amazon.

You should take note of the ones in the upper half of the top 100, such as between number one and twenty-five. Identify the products within' that range that you would fit under your brand and be able to sell. If you don't identify several, you can move on to the next twenty-five items, and continue doing so until you have a list of about five to ten products you would consider selling.

Good Product Vs. Bad Product Criteria

Before deciding to sell a product, you are going to want to make sure that what you have chosen to sell is an item that will actually earn you some profitable money. You don't want to invest hundreds of dollars on a product lead that is not going to earn you much in return. The more you can earn from a product, the better, of course. This guide is intended to help you discover what criterion identifies a good product, and what criterion identifies a bad product. This criterion is not developed from a customer's standpoint, but rather a seller's standpoint.

A good product is one that is going to have several criteria that make it a better selling opportunity for you. For starters, a good product will be one that doesn't weigh a large amount, and that is much smaller in size. This makes it easier to ship and cheaper. While you do get flat rates with Amazon FBA, those rates are likely to be much cheaper on items that cost them less to ship to customers.

Another feature of a good product is one that has an optimal selling point that will make it easy to sell several units. A product that has a higher price tag is less likely to sell as frequently and will result in you having to work harder to make money. Alternatively, you don't want one that is priced too low, because you will have to sell several units in order to make any profit. As well, you want items that have a large profit margin. This means you will make significantly more income per unit sold.

Some other features you will want to look for is a product that is durable and user-friendly. Fragile products often get damaged during shipments and that will result in you having to send out more replacement items. As well, the item being user-friendly means that the user will have an easier and better time using your product. The best way, too, is to make sure that you are getting a product that is rather unique and stands out. This will help make sure that your item gets seen in the online marketplace.

Cost wise, you want to make sure the item is something that is inexpensive to produce. This goes along with having a healthy profit margin, as well. The cheaper it is to produce, the easier it will be for you to get a startup number that will make your sales grow faster.

Also, you want to make sure that the product you are selling is something that you are passionate about and have a lot of knowledge in. The more knowledgeable you are about a product, the easier it will be for you to market and sell it. When people want to know more about that product, they will want to come back to you to get them, because they know that you know what you are talking about and that you are the person who can provide them with the best knowledge and value.

The last factor you should think about is choosing a product that is something that can be expanded on in the future. For example, many watches have been designed with interchangeable wristbands. This has a popular selling feature because consumers do not have to purchase multiple watches to get multiple styles out of their watch. Instead, they invest in a high-quality base watch and then pay a significantly lower price to purchase more wristbands so that they can mix and match their watch with their outfits each day.

If you are concerned about what a "bad" product is, it's basically anything that goes against several or all of the above points. If the product is going to be too expensive to produce, have a low-profit margin, or otherwise cost you too much money and not earn you enough profit, it is likely that it is not a good product for you to be selling. Additionally, if it is a product that you don't know much about yourself, you may want to stay away from that product. That's not to say that you absolutely should not sell that product, just that you may have a harder time marketing and promoting your product due to your minimal knowledge in the subject. You will have a harder time understanding why users would love it, and therefore you will have a harder time explaining why they should purchase your product, and not someone else's!

Market Research

Doing market research is an important part of any business, and the same rings true for Amazon FBA. This is a part of the product search you are doing, because you will need to know if your product has a strong enough market to turn you up a good profit. The ideal product is something that will be useful to a large demographic for a very strong reason. Your demographic needs to feel a strong urge to purchase this product.

There are a few ways that you can discover who your exact demographic is, and research your entire market. To start, you can think about who you think would be interested in purchasing your product. Write down the characteristics of these people, and try and identify a specific niche or demographic that your product serves. Then, you can look at existing products on the market and check out the review section of these products.

You will get an idea of who the consumers are based on their profiles and the small amounts of information you can gather from there. Their reviews themselves may also suggest information you need to know - for example, a reviewer may say "I purchased this and it helped me manage my kids' time better.

As a busy mom, it is very useful!", or whatever else they might say. By that review, you would know that the reviewer was a mom. If there were several reviews that hinted towards children being involved, then you would know that the demographic involves parents. The same rings true for any other trends you may notice among the reviewers.

You need to also consider how well these similar products are selling. Are they flying off the "shelves"? Or are they slower to sell? As well, how many other similar products are available for sale at this time? If the market is saturated, you won't want to hop on board. However, if it is unsaturated and you are confident that you have a strong competitive edge, then it may be a good idea to go forward!

Amazon has a program that will help you discover the "seller rankings" based on each product. You can actually take some time to look into this program and identify where the product lies within' the seller ranking. Ideally, the product should be 50,000 or fewer, as this suggests that the products are selling on a regular basis. Anything higher than that, especially much higher, means that they are not selling as fast and that you may not make as many sales as you would with a product on the lower end of the spectrum.

Market research is vital. It helps you discover if the market is profitable, the size of your market, and who your market actually is. This lets you know if you will make any money and how much money you may be looking at making from your product. Additionally, it helps you discover exactly who you need to target your product towards, including advertisements and marketing campaigns, product designs, and colors, and other relevant aspects of your product and sales.

Qualified Competition

You are going to want to make sure that you are able to be a qualified competitor in the marketplace. On a place like Amazon, there are hundreds of thousands of products available, and if yours doesn't "fit the bill", people will simply scroll down to find another similar product that offers better value or quality. You need to make sure that you can actually compete, and that you have a strong reason as to why people would want to purchase from you and not another seller.

Being a strong competitor comes from having a higher quality product, ideally with better features, and still at a competitive price range. Believe it or not, even if your product features several benefits over another product, if the price is too much higher then people will still go for the cheaper one even if it is not as "good" as your product is. With a marketplace like Amazon, people can quickly and easily compare products, prices, quality, and value. You need to make sure that you can compete with other existing products that are similar so that people will choose your product over someone else's.

A great way to increase your competitive edge is to read reviews on other people's products. This will give you some insight as to how the product is received and if there is room for improvement. For example, you may see reviews that consistently say something like "this tennis racket is nice, but the wires are weak and break easily". Then, you would know that if you were going to make a tennis racket that you would want to make one with stronger wires. Additionally, you would want to make sure that you emphasize this fact in your product profile so that people *knew* that you focused on this and when they see that product x, y and z had weak wires, they'll know that the ones on your tennis rackets are strong.

It is critical that you ensure that you are a qualified competitor if you are going to be entering the market with a product. No matter how amazing your product is, if you cannot compete or compare with other products, or if the market is already washed out and there is no way for you to enter with a major reason why people should purchase from you, then it is not a good idea to enter the market at all.

You must make sure that your customers feel strongly compelled to purchase your product and that they can see exactly why your product will enhance their lives, more than any other product available would.

Private Labelling

One thing you should consider with Amazon FBA is choosing products that can be private labeled. A private label means that your product can be featured with your own logo on the label and that it would be marketed as your product, not someone else's.

So, instead of selling a product that is branded by another seller or company, you can sell a product that is branded specifically for you. This is a great idea when you are planning on making an actual business out of your Amazon FBA selling, but it also takes more time for you to establish.

Ideally, if you are creating an entire brand, you want to have everything that any other brand would have. That means you would want social media presence, potentially a website, and other things associated with your brand that would help build awareness and rapport. When you are selling under your own brand, you will need to establish that you have high-quality products that are worth buying. Other brands have already established this, and have marketing teams and individuals focused on developing the brand awareness and rapport.

It may take longer to build the rapport initially, but once you do build it, you will be able to maintain it. From the point that you establish yourself as a quality company with great products, you will have an easier time selling everything in the future. Every time someone sees your brand, they will recognize you and know that they are going to be getting quality products that will fulfill their needs. Having private labeled products helps you develop this extra edge that will make your business more stable in the long term picture.

Product Creation and Fulfillment
In addition to choosing your product, you are going to need to consider product creation and fulfillment. You will only begin this process once you have picked exactly what product you want to take to the market. In this section, you are going to discover exactly how you can start getting your products created and get your orders fulfilled!

Define Your Exact Product
Before you look to get your product created and start purchasing orders, you're going to want to discover exactly

what your product is going to be. So, you know what product you want to have, but now you want to elaborate on exactly how your product is going to look, feel, and work. You want to completely outline your standards for the product, what you want it to feature, and specifications that *must* be included in the design of your product.

Manufacturers VS. Wholesalers

You are going to want to then look to see if you are going to get your product manufactured, or if you are going to purchase from a wholesaler. There are a few differences between each, so you will want to see who can fulfill your needs the best. In this section, you will learn exactly what the differences are, so that you can decide which will work best for you!

Manufacturer
A manufacturer is generally the most common route that people go, because of the versatility offered by this option. If you are looking to create a brand new product or if you want to enhance one that already exists, a manufacturer will be the one that can help you do that. As well, manufacturers have the ability to give you private labeling services, as all of the products being made are being made specifically for you.

There are some things you will need to consider about a manufacturer, however, that may be a drawback for you depending on your needs. For example, manufacturers often have fairly high "minimum order" quantities which mean you will have to order a larger number of units if you are ordering through a manufacturer.

As well, you need to be careful about where you choose to have your product manufactured because if you do not do your full research, there is a chance that you could be subjected to fraud. Finally, manufacturing your products takes significantly longer to complete in the long run.

Still, manufacturing is a great route to choose if you are looking to have unique products made for your business. As aforementioned, it allows you to private label your product easily. As well, you generally pay a really low fee for each unit since there is no "middle man" like a wholesaler. That gives you more freedom to price your product how you would like to, and have a better profit margin overall.

Something worth noting about manufacturing is that even if you are looking to develop a product that is identical to one that already exists, you can still choose a manufacturer. You do not have to go through a wholesaler just because the product has already been manufactured by someone else and for someone else. You can still purchase from a manufacturer and have these products made special for you and your business.

Wholesaler

A wholesaler is a great route to go if you want something quickly and have no desire to modify the item. Wholesalers can fulfill orders relatively fast, and can often provide you with any number of items you are looking for, no matter how big or small.

These products cannot be private labeled, but if you shop smart you can generally purchase ones that have brand names that are already recognized and well received by the industry consumers which means that you will not have to establish rapport in the marketplace.

A few drawbacks about wholesalers is that you do not have as much control over the products and their development. You cannot modify them or change them to be more suitable to yours or your consumer's needs. As well, they tend to be more expensive since a wholesaler is the middleman between you and a manufacturer.

Because of that, you will be paying more per unit, and your profit margin will be significantly lower if you choose this route. Still, you can often find good suppliers who enable you to keep your profit margin healthy and worthwhile if you take your time and thoroughly research this route.

Domestic Suppliers VS. Overseas Suppliers

The next step in choosing a supplier is deciding whether you want your supplier to be domestic or overseas. There are a few pros and cons associated with each choice, so you will want to take the time to ensure that you pick one that is going to benefit your business the best. In this chapter, you can explore what route will be the best one for you and your business.

Domestic Suppliers

Domestic suppliers are a great choice because it has a higher number of advantages than it does disadvantages, which is always a great sign! When you choose a domestic supplier, you get benefits such as having higher quality goods, better labor conditions for the workers, and less risk of fraudulent activities. As well, it is easier to communicate with the supplier to get exactly what you want, because you do not have to worry about language barriers between yourself and the supplier.

This makes it easier to get what you want, and to verify and audit manufacturers to ensure that they are providing you with quality products. Additionally, you have increased market appeal, faster shipping speeds, higher protection over your own intellectual property, and increased payment security.

Domestic suppliers have much less risk of you having a negative experience with a supplier because it is easier for you to ensure that the supplier is able to provide you with high-quality products and without running high with a risk for you overpaying or paying for something that you did not receive at all.

Still, domestic suppliers do have drawbacks that can make them less desirable for a buyer such as yourself. The con list associated with domestic suppliers consists of two main points. First, getting a product supplied to you by a domestic wholesaler means that you are going to be paying a higher cost per unit.

This is often the result of the products being higher quality, and the materials being used to make the products also being higher quality. So, it is hard to label that as a total con, when you factor in *why* you are paying more. The biggest and most prominent drawback with domestic suppliers is that you are likely to have a hard time finding a supplier who can fulfill your desired needs. Sometimes, it is even impossible to do so. However, if you can find a domestic supplier and your budget allows for it, it is highly recommended that you choose this route.

Overseas Suppliers
With overseas suppliers, you tend to face a higher number of disadvantages than you do advantages. However, many people still tend to choose overseas suppliers instead because they are convenient and often cheaper.

Ultimately, you may wish to choose an overseas supplier because they cost less per unit, there are more manufacturers to choose from, and you can often get multiple items manufactured or wholesaled from the same suppliers. This means that you can establish a relationship with your supplier and go to them for most of your expansion needs, in addition to your existing needs.

Unlike the domestic suppliers, however, you have a much higher number of disadvantages attached to overseas suppliers. For example, if your products are purchased overseas, people tend to see them as lower quality. As well, you have lower quality manufacturing standards and often lower quality products. Poor labor standards can also mean that your products are being manufactured in a place that allows for their employees to be treated poorly.

In addition to being affected by lower quality work standards and products, you also face a number of other disadvantages. When you source from overseas, you are at a higher risk for being a victim of fraud, or for having your intellectual property exposed to others, since there is little to no protection over it.

You will also have a hard time visiting your manufacturers or communicating with them to ensure that they are legitimate and able to offer you what you are actually looking for. As well, you have longer shipping waits, lower payment security, and you have to have your products clear customs and potentially pay high fees for this importation. Finally, you will also face cultural differences within' business practices that may or may not affect your experience in dealing with business dealings.

Finding a Supplier

Once you have decided what type of supplier you are going with and where you want to source them from, you will need to actually find a supplier. There are a few ways that you can find a supplier and several things you should consider before committing to one.

When you are finding a supplier, you should do a search for one online. The most reputable suppliers that will be worth doing business with will maintain an online presence of sorts. While this is not the only place that you can find manufacturers, it is a great place to start. If you are in a place like Canada or the United States of America, there are often databases that you can search on as well to discover domestic manufacturers that are available to you. You can access these databases through a simple search on any popular search engine.

You should be sure that you don't jump on the first supplier you find. You are going to want to make sure that you take your time and research the suppliers you are looking into. When you are choosing a supplier, you want to make sure that you are choosing one who is going to give you the best value for your purchase and that they are going to be able to fulfill exactly what you are looking for.

You may find several who have the ability to fulfill your exact needs, so at that point it will be up to you to discover if they can provide you with the best value possible.

When you are looking to hire a supplier, there are several things you will want to consider first. The following list of questions are things that you should ask the supplier to ensure that you are getting the best possible value for your business:

- *Is your facility able to produce the exact product that I want to order?*

- *What are you going to charge me per unit?*

- *Are there other charges I should be aware of?*

- *What is the minimum purchasing requirement for me to order?*

- *Will I receive any discounts if I purchase in larger amounts?*

- *What is your process for ensuring all of my products are high quality?*

- *If I am dissatisfied with the product I receive, what are your policies?*

- *Would I be able to purchase a single unit to ensure that it meets my standards, prior to committing to an entire order?*

- *How much extra will it cost me to have private labels or custom packaging put on my products?*

- *How long can I expect to wait to have my order filled?*

When you ask these questions, you give yourself the opportunity to go into every business deal knowing exactly what you are getting out of it. One of the main and major mistakes made by businesses in general, but especially ones that may not have any background training or education, is that they enter sales deals with expectations not being predetermined.

When you do this, it creates a world of confusion and dissatisfaction because you and your supplier may both have different ideas on how business should be conducted.

While you are doing your research on suppliers, you should take down the answers to these questions and put them on "profile pages" for each supplier. This way you can analyze the answers and compare suppliers side by side to see who is going to be the best option for you in the end.

In addition to the above questions, there are some other areas you are going to want to consider when you are researching a supplier. The following list includes things you should consider before hiring a supplier:

- *Expertise: are they highly knowledgeable about creating your desired project?*

- *Level of Control: how much control do you have over the manufacturing process, if you're choosing a manufacturer?*

- *Ability to Customize: if you're choosing a manufacturer, how many modifications can you make to a project that they can honor in the manufacturing process?*

- *Order Requirements: can they fulfill the number of units you want? And if so, will it you have to wait in between for them to replenish their supplies?*

- *Quality Control: what are their quality control standards?*

After you have asked all of your questions and considered everything about your suppliers, you should have a pretty good idea about who you want to order from.
At this point, it should be pretty clear if there is one particular supplier that seemed better than the rest. They should check out based on all of the above questions and considerations, as well as be polite and easy to work with. You don't want to choose a supplier that is too difficult to communicate with, or who doesn't seem to listen to what you are saying. Both could lead to a bad situation!

Now that you are fully aware of what is available to you, it is time to choose who you are going to use as a supplier! If you are still completely unsure and you are choosing the manufacturing route, you may wish to request a single product from a few manufacturers and then compare them to see which one physically fits your standards best. At this time, you will also gain a better idea of how each company is to do business with, and whether they listen to your wants and needs or not. A company should respond in a timely manner and listen to your needs and wants and do their best to make your experience as easy as possible.

Placing Your Order

You may find it is a bit scary to place your first order, and that's normal. Generally speaking, you're putting a lot of money into the order and you are going to end up with a lot of units on hand at Amazon. You want to make sure that those units are going to sell, and that you're going to return your investment quickly and hopefully with a significant amount of profit involved.

Before you place your order, you want to do one last check on the supplier you have chosen. Make sure that you do a good web search on them, and do your best to research their company. Do not go by the reviews on their website, as it is easy for companies to make these reviews bias. Instead, you want to go to other websites with people who have actually purchased through them, and ask how their experience actually was.
At this time, you verify that the supplier really is who they say they are and that they will be able to fulfill your orders with high-quality products as well as high-quality customer service.

Once you have verified your order, you want to place it! There are a few different ways that ordering works. For wholesalers, you may be given a membership to a website that enables you to purchase products through their website.

Or, you may be given an order form with a list of their products and prices. Then, you fill it out and e-mail it back to them. For manufacturers, it is likely that you will only get the order form, and not a membership to a website, especially if the product you are having created is unique and modified to your desires.

When you are placing your order, you have to be very thorough and ensure that you check it over a few times. Every single line and piece of information given should be accurate since you generally cannot revoke an order once it's been placed. Some businesses *may* allow a grace period of up to 24 hours following the placement of your order to make any revisions, but for the sake of convenience and time, you should just make sure your order is right the first time.

For your first order, refrain from purchasing too much stock. Even though you may be offered discounts if you purchase more, you want to make sure that you are going to actually sell your products, first. It is worth it to omit the discount and pay the slightly higher price, if applicable, for fewer products than it is to end up with too many that you cannot sell! Start small and expand from there once you know *for sure* how quickly you move your products.

Finally, once you place your order, you need to be patient. Most manufacturers and wholesalers are dealing with several businesses at once, so you are going to want to give them time to communicate with you and fulfill your order.

Remember that they are working with high volume orders, so it may take them quite some time to fulfill and ship the order. This is why you want to make sure that you are clear on what the order fulfillment times (usually) are when you are working on acquiring a supplier. It will help you know about how long you have to wait and be patient for!

Other than that, your order is pretty much done! You don't have to do much more now except wait for the order to arrive at Amazon's storage and shipping facility. In the meantime, you may wish to prepare the advertisements and get pictures of your product for the ad. At this point, it would be really beneficial to have a single unit on hand!

Amazon Fba

Chapter 3: Managing Your Product

Managing your product is fairly easy, but you are still going to want to put some work into this section. For the most part, you simply order more products and have them shipped to Amazon for Amazon to ship to the paying customers. However, there are some other aspects of product management that you will need to focus on as well, to ensure that your sales stay strong and that you are making money! This chapter will help guide you through what you need to do for that.

Ensure Product is High Quality

You want to continue managing your product to ensure that it is high quality. A high-quality product is one that will continue to sell time and again, and that consumers will be happy with purchasing it and happy to refer it to friends. You can manage this by monitoring the reviews that come in for your product.

You should watch the reviews and look for complaints, especially ones that seem to be common. Then, you can speak with your supplier and ensure that these complaints are resolved when you are ordering your next batch. If your supplier is a wholesaler, and your complaints are excessively negative, you might consider ordering from a new wholesaler.

A good rule of thumb is that you should spend more money on a lower number of higher quality units, *not* less money on a higher number of lower quality units.

If your units are not selling, you are not going to make your return. You need a product that is high quality. Trust that if you purchase the lower quantity of higher quality units, you will end up with enough return to go and purchase a larger quantity in the future. If you do the reverse, it is likely that you won't even sell out of your first order.

Maximize Your Sales

In addition to having a product available, you are going to want to put some work into making sure it actually sells. You can do this in a few ways, which you will learn about now.

- Seller and Product Reviews: people rely heavily on reviews from others to ensure products and sellers are of high quality. Encouraging reviews will help your product sell better. Amazon has a built-in feature that encourages reviewers to leave feedback on your product and your seller's profile.

- Product Photography: make sure that the photographs of your products are high quality and attractive. The better they look the more likely people will be to buy them. Refrain from having too much going on in your photographs, keep the background simple and elegant and make the product the main focus. Ensure the lighting is high quality, also!

- *Product Description: you also want to make sure that your product description is accurate and attractive. You should write in a way that appeals to your targeted demographic, which you outlined when you were having the product created. You want to use enticing words that engage the senses in a way that stimulates a person to mentally know how it would feel to own said product so that they become curious enough to want to physically own it and experience all of those feelings in real life. Make sure that you use the proper tone and vocabulary to appeal to your target audience.*

- *Amazon Keywords:* popular Amazon keywords are any words that are searched consistently and on a regular basis. You want to take full advantage of any and all keywords that are regularly searched by your targeted audience, and that would attract them easily.

- *Pricing:* you need to take a realistic look at the current market and price your items accordingly. Remember, just because your product may have many more benefits does not always justify a significantly higher price tag. Many consumers will buy a significantly cheaper product and forego some of the benefits if it means that they will be saving money.

As well as optimizing your sales through Amazon, you should work on marketing your products elsewhere, too. There are many ways you can do this, which you will learn about in the next chapter.

What to Do if Your Product Doesn't Sell

Occasionally you may run into a situation where you have done all of your research and you have tested your product but, for some reason, it still isn't selling. If that is the case, there are a few things that you can do to try and turn things around and start making more sales.

First, you want to take a look at the marketing strategies you are using. Again, you will learn more about these in the next chapter. Then, you may consider hosting a promotion to start getting sales flowing. Sometimes once you get the initial sales going, you will have a much easier time getting future sales coming in because a rapport will have been built by having a number of positive reviews in your favor.

Next, you may want to consider adjusting the price on your product. If the price is set too high, you may be driving away sales. Generally, if your product or brand is more recognized and trusted, the price will not be an issue. In the beginning, however, you may have to sell at a lower price point to make any money.

Another thing you will want to do is check your listing. Make sure that the wording is appropriate, the pictures are high quality, and that it is listed properly on Amazon. If it is properly listed, it will come up under the appropriate keywords and categories to help ensure that you are being seen by the right customers.

If all else fails and you are really struggling to clear out products, you are going to want to consider hosting a clear out sale. This means that you sell the product slightly above what you paid for the cost per unit and get rid of your entire stock. At this point, you might consider trying again with a new product. Before you do, however, ensure that you take the time to understand and learn why this product did not sell so that you can do better in the future and prevent yourself from wasting time and money.

For some people, the beginning can be difficult as you learn how to create products, product listings, and marketing campaigns to sell your products. Give yourself a chance to endure this learning curve, and in no time you will be selling products like hot cakes and you will have profit to prove it!

Chapter 4: Marketing Strategies

There isn't a lot of marketing that you need to do when you are selling on Amazon since most of your marketing is done directly through Amazon. Still, you might want to consider doing some extra marketing to increase the likelihood that your product sells and improve your ability to make sales. If you are selling on Amazon, this chapter will help you discover ways that you can market your products that won't take up a lot of your time or budget.

Social Media Marketing

Social media marketing may or may not be a route you wish to go. This option is generally more for people who are looking to start a brand and have their products private labeled so that they can have the benefit of brand recognition once they grow their brand. If you are doing this, social media marketing is a great way to go.

Social media marketing basically includes you making social profiles for your brand. You can update your statuses regularly about brand-specific information or industry-specific information. Then, when you are launching new products, you can use these platforms and your existing following to market your products to.

This will help you get information out there quickly to help you make sales. At first, you will likely have a smaller following and it may be slower going. Soon, however, your following will grow and you will have a healthy base of consistent followers to market to every time you are launching a new product or doing a promotion, or anything else that would encourage customers to buy from you.

If you are not savvy with the internet or prefer not to have to manage all of the work that goes into managing brand accounts on social media, you might consider outsourcing this. There are many people available for hire who can manage your accounts for you and post information regularly to help you get the word out there and keep your account active and your followers engaged.

Influencers

Whether you are starting a brand or not, having influencers use your products is a great way for you to make sales. You simply hire influencers from your desired demographic who have followers that match your target audience and send them a free unit of your product.

This allows them to test it and review it on their platform to their large following base, and often they can link your sales page directly to your account.

Influencers are an excellent opportunity to tap into a large following base that has already been established. As well, if you choose an influencer, they often already have the rapport and reputation built with their followers so that their followers know they can trust the influencer and their reviews. This saves you a lot of time, money and effort. Even though you are giving away product units, it can end up in you making a lot of sales.

Paid Advertisement

You might consider using paid advertisement to encourage sales on your products as well. Paid advertisements allow you to create an ad (or have a professional create one for you) and then you can promote it within' your advertising budget. The best opportunity is to promote this on social media so that you get access to several viewers at any given time.

Word of Mouth

Finally, having positive reviews on your profile and account, as well as positive reviews around the web can really help increase your sales. This is why having influencers helps: they are trusted reviewers who can encourage people to buy through you.

In addition to word of mouth on the internet, you can always let people know about your products in person, too. Then, you can link them back to your Amazon account and give them the opportunity to buy through you. The more you talk about your product and you get others talking about your product, the more people are going to want to purchase it because they will want to know what all of the chit chat is about!

Marketing your products with Amazon is not as extensive as it would be if you didn't have amazon helping you. It may seem like a lot of work, but in reality, if you simply keep up with a few areas and do a few little things here and there, it can all pay off. Even if you are not interested in putting a lot of work into marketing yourself, you can always outsource the marketing to someone else who could oversee your social media accounts, or to influencers who will share your products to their existing following. You don't have to do a lot in order to get people seeing your product.

In fact, you don't even *have* to market at all. Though, it is recommended that you do so that you maximize your visibility and increase your sales volume. After all, if people don't know you have a product available, how are they going to purchase it?

Chapter 5: Gathering Feedback

You have been learning about how important feedback is throughout this entire book, but you may be wondering how you can get feedback on your products with Amazon. Luckily, Amazon makes it incredibly easy to actually get the feedback. However, monitoring it and using it for your benefit is something that you are going to have to take care of yourself.

When you market with Amazon, they automatically send a message to your customers shortly after their purchase so that they can review your products directly on Amazon. When they do this, you will receive a rating out of 5 stars, and some customers will also give you a verbal review. Most often these written reviews only happen if the reviewer was really happy, or really upset with their purchase.

When a reviewer has taken the time to write about your product, you should always take the time to read what they have said. This gives you the opportunity to see exactly what your customers are liking about the product, and what you may be able to improve on. You should implement some form of system where you will look at the reviews on a regular basis and take notes on what is being said.

If you notice a trend in certain complaints, you can improve your products going forward. Alternatively, if you notice a consistent number of good reviews going forward on a certain aspect, you can be aware of what your consumers like and continue to provide products that match or exceed those qualities.

In addition to reviews and feedback, customers who have not yet purchased yet are actually able to leave questions on your product page. Be sure that you keep an eye on these questions. If you notice a certain question being asked a lot, you may wish to provide the answer directly in the product description so that future customers know the information without having to ask or browse through the question section to find the answer.

Even though Amazon oversees a lot of the customer service aspect of your product, you should still take the time to become involved as well. Gathering and reviewing feedback is a great way for you to gain a solid understanding of what your customers want and how you can serve them better. The more you understand what they are looking for, the easier it will be for you to come out with future products that will impress your customers and have them wanting to purchase more.

Chapter 6: Supplier Relationships

Although you may not be aware of it, supplier relationships are important no matter what type of business you are running. This is true with Amazon FBA, as well. You want to make sure that you maintain your relationship with your suppliers, as this keeps the rapport open and ensures that you will always receive the best customer service possible.

Suppliers like to deal with customers who are nice and friendly, so if you are nice and friendly, they will treat you better than others who are not. There are some things you should do in order to nurture and maintain your relationship with your suppliers, and in this chapter, you are going to explore some of those ways.

Focus on the Relationship

Ideally, you want to focus on the relationship you are developing with your supplier. While you may not be totally clear on how you can do this, especially overseas, this part is actually simple. It mostly requires you to be polite and kind, and set yourself up so that you are an enjoyable client to work with. Suppliers enjoy working with clients who are friendly and nice, and who are able to take the stiff business side out of things, within' reason.

You don't want to be unprofessional, but you should still be friendly and respectful. When you do this, you make yourself a pleasant client to work with, which ends up making the supplier even more pleasant to work with. Generally speaking, they love working with people who are polite and easy to work with. This makes their job a lot easier, and it makes your job a lot easier, too!

Mutually Beneficial Relationships

Remember that your relationship with your supplier should be viewed as a team. You are both there to help fulfill the need of creating and providing a product that will serve your client. If you didn't have a supplier, your business wouldn't thrive. If your supplier didn't have a client (you), their business wouldn't thrive.

You both rely on each other to keep your businesses running, therefore you should be prepared to view the relationship as a mutually beneficial relationship. Treat your supplier with respect and kindness, and you should expect that they will do the same. One is not better than the other, and no one should be getting treated unfairly in the agreement. Both of you should be benefitting and neither should be feeling as though they have been taken advantage of in the relationship.

Opening the Door for Opportunities

When you have a high-quality relationship with your suppliers, it opens the door for a lot of opportunities. Clients to suppliers that are friendly and kind and who share a relationship with the supplier often get rewarded for this.

They are more likely to receive higher quality products, and the supplier is often excited to give the seller exclusive first opportunities to work with their new technologies. This means that when the supplier is able to offer new and better services, they will be more likely to share it with you first.

This is a great opportunity to have because it means that you are going to have new cutting edge products to share with your clients before anyone else does. As well, if you maintain a loyal relationship with your supplier, they will be more likely to provide you with better deals or discounts in the future.

The Relationship Goes Both Ways

When you are building a relationship with your supplier, you need to remember that the relationship goes both ways. Having this in mind, make sure that you are being loyal and kind to your suppliers in the same way that you want them to be loyal and kind to you. Remember that without you, they have no customers, without them you have no products.

Make sure that you are nurturing your relationships and offering fair and valuable agreements to your suppliers so that you are both benefiting from the relationship. This will make them more likely to want to give you better service, the same way that their respect and loyalty makes them more likely to give you better service, too.

If you are looking to further enhance your relationship as well as save money, you may want to speak with your supplier to see what you can do in order to reduce the costs. This saves them time and investment, and saves you money as well. Your supplier and you will both benefit from this, so it is worth asking and looking into!

Accepting Accountability

It is important that you are willing to accept accountability in your relationship with your supplier. In the next section, you will learn about the importance of clearly outlined agreements and penalties. With this being a two-way relationship, naturally you are going to be prone to the penalties just like your supplier will be if anything goes wrong. It is important that you accept accountability in the relationship and that you are not trying to pass the blame.

This is part of having a positive and strong relationship with your supplier. If you are unwilling to accept accountability, your supplier is not going to enjoy working with you because it makes working with you more difficult. Because of this, it is important that you are ready and willing to take responsibility and be held accountable for your own actions and situations. Even though it doesn't always have a positive outcome for you, in the long run, it will keep your relationship stronger with your supplier which is a positive outcome.

Clear Agreements

A strong part about having a productive relationship with your business is having clear agreements with your supplier. Clear agreements will enable you to be able to know exactly what you can expect from each other. It helps with knowing who should be held accountable for what, and what you need to do in order to fulfill your end of the relationship.

As well, you will know exactly what you should expect from your supplier and how to tell if *they* need to be held accountable for not holding up their end of the deal. Clear agreements should be outlined before you go into a relationship with one another, and they should be agreed upon by both parties.

It is important that both parties are fully aware of what they are supposed to do in order to maintain their side of the agreement, to make sure that there are no discrepancies or issues within' your relationship. Having clear agreements will make your relationship with your supplier much smoother and will prevent you from running into troubles down the line that may or may not affect your business and profitability.

Clear Penalties

Within' the agreements of your contract, you should clearly outline what the penalties will be if either party fails to uphold their end of the deal.

So, if you do something wrong or outside of the terms of agreement, you will know exactly what the penalty would be as a result of that action. As well, if the supplier does something that lies outside of the terms of agreement, they will also know what will happen as a result of their own action. This helps ensure that you can hold each other accountable and that proper action will be taken to keep both parties being treated fairly for the duration of your relationship together.

Being Clear and Open

At all times during your relationship with your supplier, you should be clear and open with your business. You should also expect that they be clear and open as well. What that means is, if you are having a change made to one of your orders, if you are struggling with something, or if anything to do with your side of the bargain is not being fulfilled, you should talk about that.

If the supplier has a change made, if they are unable to fulfill a part of the order, or if anything is happening that compromises their ability to fulfill their side of the deal, they should also be able to be clear and open with you in order to let you know what is going on. Furthermore, you should expect that they be clear and open with you.

Planning Ahead

It is important that you always plan ahead when you are placing orders and working with your supplier. Ensure that you order with plenty of time for them to fulfill your order and provide you with what you need so that you are not feeling pressed for time. If you order too late and your order does not arrive when you need it, recognize that this is a result of your own tardiness, and therefore it is you who should be held accountable, not the supplier.

When you realize that you are being held accountable for these things, do not try and blame the supplier or pass the blame to someone else to get out of your respective penalty. Instead, own the accountability of your action and ensure that you do better in the future.

As well, you should make sure that you have a backup supplier on hand to help ensure that if anything goes wrong, you have somewhere else you can go to get your orders fulfilled. Doing this will help in the event that your supplier ends up short staffed, or without the resources to fulfill your order, or your entire order. That way, your business will not suffer as a result.

Renegotiate Contracts Annually

An important thing you should be doing with your business is renegotiating contracts with your suppliers on an annual basis. Doing this will help you tremendously when it comes to keeping your contracts clean and efficient.

Many things can change over the course of a year, so having your business contracts renegotiated ensures that they are up to date and reflect the most recent practices being undertaken. This will help protect both you and your supplier, as it will keep everything updated and help you continue to keep accountability clear and outlined.

It will also make your business ordeals easier overall, as it will enable you to always know exactly what is expected of you, and will help your supplier always know exactly what is expected of them, as well. Doing this is really just a part of having strong housekeeping skills and ensuring that both you and your supplier are getting the best possible deals from your contract.

Expect Honesty

You should always expect honesty when you are working with a supplier, and furthermore, you should reward honesty. If your supplier has anything they need to warn you about, such as being short staffed for a certain period of time, broken equipment, or anything else, you should be informed in a timely manner.

You should expect that you will always be kept up to date with anything that affects your business and your orders. As well, you should make sure that you are always open and kind when you are receiving this honesty, especially when it comes in a very timely manner. You should always thank your supplier for letting you know and be kind to them in return. Remember, this is affecting their business, too.

It is worth noting that these types of situations are the reason why it is so important to have a backup supplier who can help you in the event that your regular supplier cannot fulfill orders for you. You should already have this backup supplier verified and ensure that they will be able to fulfill orders and maintain the high quality that you are used to in your business. This will make sure that your own customers are never affected by an issue with suppliers.

Maintaining your relationship with your suppliers and doing

this basic housekeeping work may seem a bit difficult, but it really isn't. It is an important part of running a business and keeping it running smoothly. It will really help you in getting your customer's needs taken care of, and earning you a profit in return.

While it does take extra time to maintain these relationships, you will find that it will be highly worthwhile in the end. Having positive relationships with your suppliers has many benefits that money simply cannot buy.

It makes your relationships more enjoyable, increases the value you gain from your supplier, and keeps everything within' your own business running smoothly. There are several reasons as to why you should be focused on maintaining these relationships, and doing so will help you succeed and make even more profit in your own company.

Conclusion

Starting an Amazon FBA business is not as hard as it may sound, and the work that goes into it is generally easy. While there are some steps you need to cover to ensure you are doing it properly, having it done right will keep you earning profit time and time again.

There are a few areas that you need to consider when you are building your Amazon FBA business, as you truly are building a business and you need to ensure that you run it as such. You should always be professional and ensure that you or your outsourcing is vigilant about keeping up with everything.

I hope that this book was able to provide you solid insight on how you can start your own Amazon FBA business and earn money with it. This book is aimed at helping you build a lucrative business opportunity that will have you earning a wealth of profits. Should you decide that you want to be more withdrawn from the company and simply earn profit from it, you can always outsource the work to other parties so that is completed and you continue to benefit from it as a result.

Amazon FBA is truly a powerful business to get into. These days, everyone does their shopping online. While brick and mortar stores are wonderful, having an online business is easy, and gives you wide open access to a much larger audience. Getting into this business is something that will serve you for years to come, as long as you maintain it properly.

The next step for you is to decide what product you are going to take to market. Then, you can start finding a supplier and either have the product made for you or shipped for you. At that point, you can start marketing your product. Then, you want to build a powerful advertisement page on Amazon and ensure that your keywords are proper.

Finally, you want to make sure that you do all of the proper housekeeping by managing feedback and supplier relationships so that you can be sure that your business will serve for years to come.

Again, it may seem difficult at first, but if you take it one step at a time and lay down a solid foundation, you will be able to easily create a business that will have plenty of profit and opportunities for you to enjoy.

You can go virtually anywhere with your business on Amazon FBA, which is one of the best parts of it. You can expand your business as large as you want and earn as much as you'd like simply by repeating the process within' this book over and over and over again.

If you enjoyed this book and felt that it added value to your life,

Amazon Fba

I kindly ask that you please take a moment to review it on Amazon. Your feedback would be greatly appreciated.

Thank you, and enjoy your new Amazon FBA business!

www.ingramcontent.com/pod-product-compliance
Lightning Source LLC
Chambersburg PA
CBHW061221180526
45170CB00003B/1108